# COPERNICUS

The Discovery of the Heliocentric Revolution

Written by Mélanie Mettra
Translated by Rose Brichard

History **50MINUTES**.com

# NICOLAUS COPERNICUS AND THE HELIOCENTRIC REVOLUTION

- **Born:** 19 February 1473 in Toruń, Poland
- **Died:** 24 May 1543 in Frauenburg, modern-day Frombork, Poland
- **Major achievement:** formulating a heliocentric model of the solar system

The name Copernicus is synonymous with a major turning point in the history of astronomy. For fourteen centuries, planetary observation and calculations had been based on Aristotelian and Ptolemaic theory, which held that the Earth was stationary in the middle of a finite universe, orbited by the other planets and extra-terrestrial objects in a realm beyond which lived monsters, gods and angels. Copernicus changed all of this forever, introducing a new system which harboured the seeds of a revolution.

The early 17th century is marked by monumental change. Equipped with new technologies, explorers took to the seas in search of new passages to new lands. While Copernicus was studying in Krakow, Christopher Columbus (1450/1451-1506) discovered America. At the same time, humanism was transforming the intellectual sphere, cultivating a thirst for knowledge driven by Europe's rediscovery of its antique roots and enriched by the intellectual explosion from the medieval East. The Roman Catholic Church was equally shaken to its core by the Protestant Reformation, and found its second wind through its own counter-reformation.

This period, characterised by a cultural return to antiquity, is nonetheless marked a profound separation from the intellectual traditions for which Claudius Ptolemy (100-170 AD) was responsible. He was a true polymath; a mathematician, geographer and astronomer who established precedents in geography and astronomy which would last for an astonishing length of time. However, the discovery of America showed the cracks in his geographic model and Nicolaus Copernicus too would transform Ptolemy's theory of the heavens with the shocking proposition that the Earth was not immobile. Further still, Copernicus hypothesised a universe in which the Earth turned on its own axis and orbited the sun, which replaced the Earth as the planetary system's central entity. These are the only elements which differentiate Copernican theory from Ptolemy's model, therefore the two hypothetical systems remain largely similar. Nevertheless, Copernicus was at the origin of a revolution which would, across the five centuries which followed his life and work, radically alter our understanding of the universe. This revolution occurred in several stages, from Galileo (Italian astronomer and physicist, 1564-1642) to Kepler (German astronomer, 1571-1630), from Kepler to Newton (English physicist, mathematician and astronomer, 1642-1727) and from Newton to Einstein (American physicist, 1879-1955).

# BIOGRAPHY

## A HUMANIST EDUCATION

Nicolaus Copernicus was born on 19 February 1473 in Toruń, a city in Royal Prussia in the heart of the Kingdom of Poland. He was the youngest of four children and his father, a rich merchant from Krakow, was attracted to Toruń by its flourishing commerce as part of the Hanseatic League. Copernicus was orphaned at just ten years old and taken to live with his maternal Uncle Lukas Watzenrode (1447-1512), a highly cultured man who was renowned for his military prowess and above all for his position as Bishop of Warmia (Ermland).

Having been tutored by the future chaplain to Pope Leon X (1475-1521), Bernard Sculteti (1455-1518), the 18-year-old Nicolaus Copernicus was sent by his uncle to the University of Krakow to study theology, canon law and liberal arts. It was under the teaching of Albert de Brudzewo (Polish astronomer, 1445-1497) that Copernicus learned the rudiments of astronomy. In 1496, he left for Italy to continue his studies at the University of Bologna where he continued to specialise in law and philosophy. However, in Bologna he made the acquaintance of Domenico Maria Novara (Italian astronomer, 1454-1504), with whom he made numerous astronomical observations and discovered the philosophical and scientific literature which existed on the subject.

Meanwhile, his uncle was appointed as Canon at Frombork Cathedral. After returning to Poland to take orders,

Copernicus left once again for Italy, this time to study in Padua. There, he focussed his studies on medicine, though still managed to earn the title of doctor in canon law in May 1503. He then returned home to Poland, where he was to stay for almost all of his life until his death.

## A DIVERSE CAREER PATH

As canon, Copernicus had great economic and political responsibility. As a doctor, he cared for his uncle the Bishop of Warmia. Furthermore, Copernicus assumed administrative responsibilities within the Prince-Bishopric of Warmia, his duties including land allocation, assisting settlers and representing the Chapter at Royal Prussian state assemblies.

When Poland went to war with the knights of the Teutonic Order, Copernicus fought in the conflict and was forced to flee Frombork during an attack in January 1520. He also organised the city of Olsztyn's defence as a military commander.

Meanwhile, Copernicus was also writing an important paper on economic and monetary reform – *De monete cutende ratio*, ie "On the Minting of Coin". In this work, Copernicus writes with great scientific rigour on the importance of monetary value in relation to gold and silver. He also expressed an early version of what would come to be known as "Gresham's law", whereby bad money drives out good money; that is, if two currencies are produced at the same time, the more valuable of the two will be stockpiled and cease to circulate while the less valuable will remain.

All these activities did not distract Copernicus from his true passion - astronomy. Every time Copernicus made a journey, he observed the heavens. Furthermore, he commissioned the construction of a tower near Frombork Cathedral which would house an observatory. His wide reading of Greek, Latin and Arab texts and his own investigations led him to question the Ptolemaic astronomical model which had prevailed for over one thousand years. Ptolemy's geocentric system held that the Earth was situated at the centre of the universe and orbited by the other planets, something which was assrted through a series of complex adjustments. Copernicus, however, theorised a simpler heliocentric model. He made these momentous discoveries quietly and discreetly. His book *De revolutionibus orbium coelestium* – "On the Revolutions of the Heavenly Spheres" was almost certainly completed in 1530, yet remained unpublished until 1543 when it was printed in Nuremberg a few weeks before Copernicus died. His friend and disciple Georg Joachim von Lauchen, also known as Rheticus (Polish astronomer, 1514-1576) tried to distribute and diffuse the work of his master; not Copernicus himself. The book, which would in time lead to the major paradigm shift of the Copernican revolution, was initially met with little success. Its true value was only exposed when Tycho Brahe (Danish astronomer, 1546-1601), Galileo and Johannes Kepler used it as the basis for their own scientific deductions and discoveries.

Copernicus died from a brain haemorrhage in May 1543.

## A NEW TOMB FOR COPERNICUS

According to tradition, canons are buried in their own cathedrals. However, for centuries, Copernicus' tomb could not be located in Frombork. On 4 November 2005, after new research helped locate his burial site, archaeologists found his remains at the foot of the Holy Cross altar. The body was identified as that of Copernicus through analysis of the skull and tufts of hair belonging to one of the skeletons found there. Copernicus' body was reburied in his own cathedral on 22 May 2010 after being honoured by Józef Kowalczyk (Polish Bishop born 1938) in a mass dedicated to the occasion.

# CONTEXT

## POLAND, KINGDOM OF CHAOS

Ever since the Christian Kingdom of Poland was created in the 5$^{th}$ century AD, neighbouring states had viewed it as a target for conquest and invasion. Not only the Holy Roman Empire of the German Nation, but the Prussians and Lithuanians all made regular attempts to seize the land acquired by the Polish kings of the Piast Dynasty (roughly 960AD-1370) or support other invasion efforts. Throughout the 12$^{th}$ century, the kingdom was therefore divided into smaller vulnerable duchies.

In the 13$^{th}$ century, it was the Mongols' turn to invade the lands dominated by the Knights of the Teutonic Order, coming to the rescue of the Duke of Mazovia who was battling against the Prussians. Polish unity was largely fostered through the growing influence of the Church's, an influence exerted through local bishoprics which were the driving force in the community. The reign of Casimir III (1309-1370) marks a turning point in Polish politics: he succeeded in driving out the burdensome presence of the Teutonic Knights and conquer new territories which were to be distributed among farming settlers, in turn improving their standard of living. It was also under his reign that Polish industry, commerce and its cultural renown developed, the latter thanks to the founding of the University of Krakow. When the king died, the throne was initially passed on to his nephew Louis of Hungary (1326-1382) and then Louis' daughter, Jadwiga of Anjou (1372-1399). In 1386, Jadwiga married the King of

Lithuania who became King of Poland under the name of Ladislas II of Jagiellon (1352-1434).



### THE TEUTONIC ORDER

The Teutonic Order was created between 1191 and 1198 during the third crusade at Acre in the Holy Land (Israel). It was originally founded to help German Christians on pilgrimage to the Holy Land, but the brothers of the House of Saint Mary soon formed a military order with the goal of protecting the Holy Land. During the 13th century, they moved to Northern Europe to lead campaigns against pagan populations. They conquered Prussian, Polish and Lithuanian territories and founded cities (including Toruń) and a Teutonic monastic state. However, being constantly at war with their neighbours meant that by the mid-16th century their zone of control was limited to West Prussia, a vassal of the Polish Crown. The Teutonic Order was divided through the Protestant Reformation, and went into decline until it was eventually dissolved by Napoleon I (French Emperor, 1769-1821) in 1809. It was reformed in the early 20th century and these days dedicates itself to charitable works and education.

The Jagiellon dynasty (1377-1572) presided over Poland, Lithuania and part of Ukraine and the Teutonic Knights were their main enemy. They occupied Poland's Northern coast and as such Ladislas II and his successor Casimir IV (1427-1492) battled with the Order for more than half of the 15th century before finally imposing the Peace of Thorn in 1466 which allowed them access to the Baltic Sea.

Aside from this conflict, the vast Kingdom of Poland was faced with Russian, Ottoman and Germanic invasions. In the early 16th century it became a constitutional monarchy in which laws, tax increases and the military were voted on by a legislative body which consisted of the King, the Senate (a body of highly-placed military and religious dignitaries), representatives of local assemblies and the nobility. While the Kingdom was largely divided along linguistic, ethnic, religious and civil lines, resulting in near-constant warfare between different duchies, the 16th century marked the beginning of Poland's golden age. Enriched by the renaissance, Poland became a hub of intellectualism and knowledge diffused by Polish-speaking scholars, fostering a new form of national unity.

## HUMANISM AND THE REFORMATION

While linguistic, cultural and religious diversity was in many ways an obstruction to establishing national unity, it endowed the Polish people with a certain tolerance which was further developed through the spread of thinking from the Renaissance and humanism. First developed in Italy, these two movements, the former artistic and the latter intellectual, are both characterised by a return to ancient sources and antiquity, whether with regards to architecture, painting, sculpture or indeed Greek and Arab philosophy. This new inspiration gave birth to an effervescent culture which spread throughout all of Europe largely due to its network of universities. As such, a whole new generation of scholars and artists emerged, who established a following through travelling between universities and thanks to the huge increase in print literature with the invention of the Gutenberg Press (invented by German printer Gutenberg, 1397-1468) in Mayence.

Between 1500 and 1530, the University of Krakow became a renowned intellectual centre, particularly after its reform under the Jagiellon reign. The university counted many astronomer-mathematicians among its academic workforce, including Lawrence of Raciborz (1381-1448), Piotr Lozmierza, (roughly 1430-1474) who developed a method for calculating longitude, and Albert Brudzewski. The latter designed popular astronomic tables calculated for the Krakow meridian and was the first to shed light on the contradictions of geocentrism. Lastly, Martin Biem of Olkusz (1470-1540) was a reporter to the fifth Lateran Council (1512-1517) regarding plans to reform the calendar based on the most up-to-date astronomical calculations, to which Copernicus himself contributed. All of these figures helped build strong scientific foundations on which Copernicus was to base his future work and discoveries.

It was during this same period that a new religious movement emerged, with August Monk Martin Luther's (1483-1546) criticisms of Catholicism at its source. This new wave of religious thinking, which would trigger the Protestant Reformation, was fuelled by humanism, a school of thought which advocates rereading texts and a personal relationship with one's faith. The Reformation spread through Poland much in the same way as it did in other Northern European countries; largely disseminated among the nobility by figures such as Jan Łaski (1499-1560), a Polish bishop with close ties to Ulrich Zwingli (Swiss theologian and pastor, 1484-1531) and Desiderius Erasmus (Dutch theologian and humanist, 1467-1536), whose library Łaski later purchased. This new religion preached great tolerance and was officially recognised by the princes of Poland in the 1573 Warsaw Pact which established the Warsaw Confederation. This led the kingdom to become renowned as a refuge for Christian dissidents. This penchant for Protestantism died out at the end of the 17th century when the newly founded Jesuit Order, born of the new Catholic Counter-Reformation, turned Polish elites back towards Catholicism, the majority of the civilian population having remained attached to the Catholic Church.

## THE DISCOVERY OF AMERICA

The Northern-European cultural environment of humanism laid favourable foundations for a new wave of scientific thought of which Copernicus would become a symbol, but it would also trigger a revolution. While Copernicus focussed on astronomy at a theoretical level, Christopher Columbus applied these theories to reality and set out on a quest to reach the Indies by crossing the Atlantic.

Columbus followed in the steps of great Portuguese explorers such as Henry the Navigator (Prince of Portugal, 1394-1460) and Bartolomeu Dias (explorer, roughly 1450-1500) when he attempted his momentous journey in the hope of opening up a new route to Asia. His voyage was financed by the Spanish royals Isabella I of Castile (1451-1504) and Ferdinand II of Aragon (1452-1516). Instead of reaching the Indies, Columbus came across a new continent and in doing so gave way to an unprecedented rush to find and exploit natural materials; something which would transform global commerce. This great discovery affected Copernicus in two ways. Firstly, at a scientific level, it demonstrated the importance of astronomy in concretising the intellectual currents of the time. Secondly, the new passage to Asia would little by little eclipse the medieval Hanseatic League of traders, thus affecting Copernicus' merchant family

# HIGHLIGHTS

## THE PTOLEMAIC MODEL

It was during the 16th century that Ptolemy's model of the universe was finally challenged. Ptolemy was a Greek scholar of Alexandrian origin who was a mathematician, geographer and astronomer - he even invented instruments to observe the heavens with. The system put forward in Ptolemy's *Geography* (roughly 150 AD) would remain the generally accepted geographic model until America was discovered and the discipline itself was radically reformed by the Gymnase Vosgien (cultural and scientific association) at Saint-Dié-des-Vosges under the Duke of Lorraine around 1500. This period of the early 16th century would also see Copernicus challenge Ptolemy's system of astronomy.

The Ptolemaic model, as outlined in *Almagest* (2nd century AD), is based on three principles: a trigonometric method of calculating distance, tables of chords used to locate planets and stars and lastly his cosmology, i.e. model of the universe. Ptolemy's cosmology was largely inspired by the Aristotelian model (Aristotle - Greek scholar, 384-322 BC), and it was this part of Ptolemy's scientific treatise that Copernicus called into question.

According to Ptolemy, the Earth was immobile and situated at the centre of the planetary system, with the other planets, the moon and the sun spinning around it in a perfectly circular motion and at a uniform speed. However, this theory could not account for certain observed phenomena, namely that planets seemed to exhibit slowed-down or even retrograde motion; a planet which usually moves eastward may sometimes appear to travel westward before returning to its normal course. Ptolemy tried to explain this phenomenon by incorporating eccentrics, epicycles and the equant which are explained below:

- Eccentrics: the Earth is at the centre of a circle known as a deferent, however, planets orbit the Earth on a circular path whose centre-point - known as the eccentric - is located some distance from the Earth.
- Epicycles: in addition to a planet's circular motion around the eccentric, it also makes smaller circular movements known as epicycles, whose centre is situated on the eccentric circle.
- The Equant Point: a planet's speed is uniform in relation to a third point on the radius known as the equant point, and not in relation to the centre of the deferent (the Earth) or the eccentric.

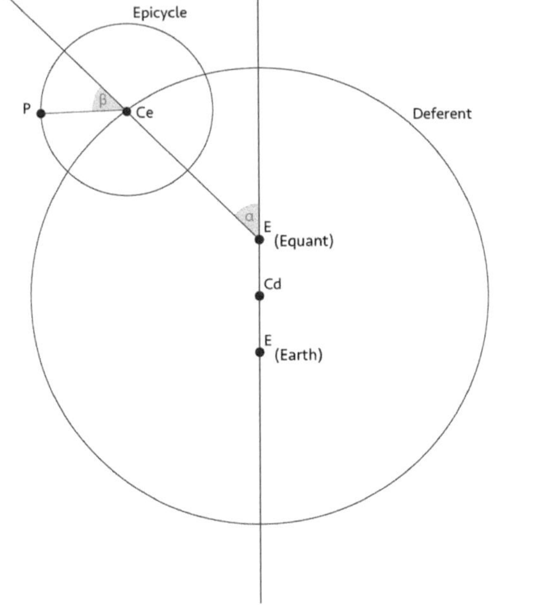


Diagram of planetary trajectory according to Ptolemy's model.

This system, based on the simple principle of an immobile Earth at the centre of the planetary system, suddenly becomes much more complex when trying to account for observed reality.

## COPERNICAN OBSERVATIONS

Copernicus was part of a long and rich tradition of astronomy from ancient to medieval times. His work was based on Greek, Arab and Western philosophy and astronomy, using methods and instruments which had not evolved greatly since ancient times.

In his work *De revolutionibus*, Copernicus mentions his use of the quadrant, which is without a doubt the oldest astronomical instrument known to man. A quadrant is a square instrument which allows the user to calculate angles to measure the position of an observed object, its movements as time passes and its ecliptic (the apparent path of an object in the celestial sphere).

Photo of a quadrant housed in the Copernicus Museum in Frombork

Another instrument Copernicus used was the armillary sphere - a scale model of the celestial globe in which each ecliptic is represented by an armillary (a ring). The instrument shows planetary movement around the Earth. The Copernican globe is highly complex, and was the first to situate the sun at the centre of the solar system. It is composed of circles representing time zones and meridians as well as a system of pins, needles and screws which shows precise astronomical positions.

Sketch of an armillary sphere taken from Diderot and d'Alembert's Encyclopédie

Lastly, Copernicus used a parallactic instrument known as a triquetrum or parallactic instrument, constructed from two fixed posts and one mobile arm. Two of the posts are exactly the same length, while the third is equal to the hypotenuse of the right-angled triangle formed by the other two posts (namely the longest side of the triangle). It allowed the user to calculate the distance to the observed object and seems to be one of Copernicus' most-used pieces of equipment.

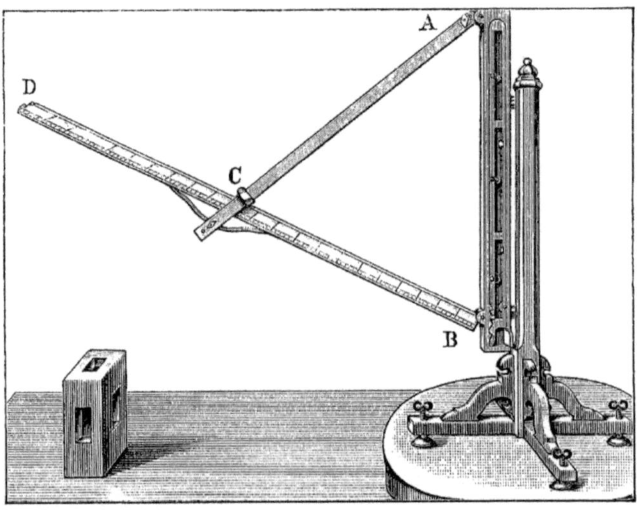


Sketch of a triquetrum

From his tower in Frombork, Copernicus also used astronomical tables which indicated the time and angle at which a heavenly body could be seen from a specific location. Regular record-keeping and study of such tables allowed him to study the movements of planets and stars in the celestial sphere. The first tables were produced by Ptolemy and updated by medieval astronomers, first in the Arab world and then in the West. These tables were revised in the 13th century at the request of King Alfonso X of Castile (1221-1284), showing not only the moon and other visible planets' movements but also different astronomical events such as eclipses and conjunctions. Copernicus in turn made his own tables and allowed his successors to make observations with increasing precision through his heliocentric model. Such observations and calculations were not only important for scientific understanding of the heavens but for navigating the seas.

## WHAT ABOUT ASTROLOGY?

In both ancient and medieval times, astronomy and astrology were inextricably linked. While the quest for understanding the world around us was driven by scientific curiosity, the role played by more mundane elements in this pursuit should also be noted. The heavens were considered as the realm of angels or as the backdrop for representations of mythology - like the Milky Way Galaxy being the milk flowing from Greek goddess Hera's breast as she suckles the baby Heracles. Above all, the sky was used to predict the future. Medieval Arab astronomers were first and foremost astrologers who used their understanding of celestial mechanics to predict individual destinies or political events. In fact, Copernicus was at the forefront of new scientific understanding which would break with traditional religious and spiritual concepts of the earth at the centre of the universe, the sky as the realm of gods and angels and the world of purgatory. This in turn would lead to the definitive separation of astronomy and astrology.

## THE NEW HELIOCENTRIC PLANETARY SYSTEM

Due to the few instruments Copernicus had at his disposal and the basic nature of astronomical observations of the time, Copernicus' work was largely mathematical. Identifying Copernicus' exact influences is difficult, but he undoubtedly owes a great deal to his forebears. Already in ancient times, Aristarchus of Samos (Greek astronomer and mathematician, 310-230 BC) proposed that the sun was at the centre of the planetary system. Hicetas of Syracuse (Greek philosopher and astronomer, 4th century BC) and Heracleides Ponticus (Greek philosopher, 4th century BC) equally suggested that the Earth turned alone on its own axis while the other planets orbited the sun. Nicole Oresme (French prelate and scholar, 1325-1382) also theorised a system of daily planetary movements.

As such, Copernicus's idea was not totally original. However, Copernicus himself was most concerned by the Ptolemaic system's imprecise nature and its inability to account for observed phenomena despite its complexity. Copernicus' first work on astronomy was *Nicolai Copernici de hypothe-*

*sibus motuum caelestium a se constitutis commentariolus* - "Nicolaus Copernicus, a Sketch of his Hypothesis for the Celestial Motions" which first appeared in 1514. In this work, he does little more than outline his principles - that the Earth is not at the centre of the universe; each celestial body has its own unique orbit path; the sun is the centre of the solar system, and the Earth spins on its own axis. He would go on to develop this treatise in his only printed text *De revolutionibus orbium coelestium.*

Aristotle and Ptolemy conceived of the universe as a series of solid spheres, including the one in which our solar system existed. The Earth was found in centre of it all and the planets appeared in this order: the moon, Mercury, Venus, the sun, Mars, Jupiter and Saturn. Copernicus on the other hand proposed that the sun was at the centre of the system, orbited by the planets in the following order: Mercury, Venus, Earth, Mars, Jupiter and Saturn. The moon does not figure in the Copernican model since it orbits the Earth and is therefore independent of the other planets. The system carried the advantage of being able to explain retrograde motion without having to resort to Ptolemaic epicycles or more importantly the equant point which Copernicus considered to be a mathematical aberration. Apparent planetary retrograde motion is in fact due to the Earth itself; those planets situated beyond the Earth take more time to orbit the sun therefore the Earth regularly overtakes them in its own orbit, giving the impression that they are moving backwards. Copernicus also linked a planet's distance from the sun to its orbital period, i.e. the time taken for a planet to complete one full circle around the sun. He argued that the further away a planet is from the sun, the longer its orbital period.

## THE EARTH'S MOTION

Copernicus went beyond presenting a new heliocentric system, he also demonstrated the Earth's motion. Like the idea of heliocentrism, Copernicus' position was not totally original, having already been presented by two other people.

First of all, the German Cardinal Nicholas of Cusa (1401-1464) theorised an infinite universe which therefore had no centre; the Earth, like the other planets, rotates on its own axis. While Nicholas of Cusa later retracted the more radical aspects of his theory and placed the earth back in the centre of a celestial sphere, his position regarding the Earth's motion remained unchanged. His thinking was echoed by other humanists such as Giovanni Pico della Mirandola (Italian humanist and theologian, 1463-1494), Jakob Ziegler (German humanist and theologian, 1471-1549) and Celio Calcagnini (1479-1541). Calcagnini was a diplomat in service to the papacy, a humanist of great renown and a friend of Erasmus who also argued that the earth rotated daily on its own axis in a finite universe. He therefore departed from the notion that the whole universe turned around an immobile planet Earth every 24 hours, at what would be break-neck speed.

Since Copernicus had established that the sun was at the centre of the universe, the Earth - along with the other planets - was therefore constantly engaged in a dual motion which Copernicus compared to that of a spinning top. This duality explained not only the seasons which reflect the earth's orbit of the sun, but the difference between day and night as a result of the Earth rotating on its own axis.

## THE LIMITS OF THE COPERNICAN SYSTEM

Though Copernicus revolutionised astronomy with his heliocentric system and his explanation of the earth's motion, his model still retained several Ptolemaic principles:

- planetary orbits are circular
- the solar system is encapsulated in a sphere scattered with motionless stars
- the planets are solid spheres

The limited technology available to Copernicus is without a doubt responsible for his assumption that stars are immobile; the relationship between distance and apparent motionlessness had not yet been established.

Furthermore, the Copernican system relies on an almost Ptolemaic level of complexity to explain planets' circular orbits. His belief that planets moved in perfect circles prevented him from fully understanding observed retrograde and slowed-down motion. Copernicus was forced to conserve Ptolemy's theory of epicycles in his model.

## PHILOSOPHICAL REASONING

One characteristic which draws together both medieval and modern texts is the fine line drawn between science and philosophy; Copernicus' work is no different. In his texts,

Copernicus passes smoothly from presenting his scientific theses to developing a philosophy based on Aristotle's Rhetoric. He also carefully deconstructs any arguments which could be levelled against him and responds to each by showing that his system not only offers answers to thus-far unsolvable questions but simplifies pre-existing models. From there he moves into theology, arguing that God is perfection and simplicity; so too is all creation, made in His image.

The Copernican revolution in some ways addresses the philosophical questions regarding the distinction between the observer and the observed. While Greek philosophers argued that appearances can be deceiving, they did not go as far as to assert that observations differ depending on the location they are made from, a notion which posits true relativity. This concept introduces the idea that invisible or imperceptible realities do exist - such as the earth's motion - and can be detected through scientific investigation.

Overall, the Copernican system is the product of logical deduction and calculation based on scientific reasoning; much more than mere observation and experience.

# IMPACT

## A MIXED RECEPTION AMONG REFORMATIONISTS

Though Copernicus had without a doubt finished his book by 1514, it remained unpublished until 1543 and was only distributed with the help of Copernicus' only disciple Rheticus. Rheticus outlined Copernican theory in his own work *Narratio Prima* (*First Discourse*) published in 1540 before dedicating himself to printing and distributing *De revolutionibus*. He first tried in Wittenberg, Germany where the book was refused before he found a willing publisher in Nuremberg. In this time of the Counter-Reformation when the Catholic Church was quick to condemn any challenge to its doctrines, Copernicus seems to have maintained some astonishing immunity from the Church's wrath.

The first objections come instead from other thinkers, particularly from certain reformationists. Martin Luther himself was known to have mentioned and quickly rejected a certain astronomer's farfetched hypotheses before *De revolutionibus* was even published. It is, however, unclear whether he was referring to Copernicus in doing so. Rheticus' guardian Philipp Melanchthon (German humanist, 1497-1560) was the first to challenge Copernican theory. When Rheticus showed Melancthon the first draft of his own book which outlined the heliocentric hypothesis, Melancthon rejected the idea that the Earth orbited the sun on the grounds that it contradicted Scripture which, on several occasions, makes reference to the Earth as stationary and the sun as mobile.

He was nonetheless fascinated by astrology and admired the Copernicus' methodology and the quality of his calculations. Melancthon eventually helped finance a new set of planetary tables based on the Copernican method.

Another renowned reformer John Calvin (1509-1564) denounced those who rejected geocentrism, though he never condemned Copernicus or his work directly.

Not all reformers rejected Copernicus' theses. The German theologian Andreas Osiander (1498-1552) revised and wrote the preface for *De revolutionibus*. He is also almost certainly responsible for the lack of uproar towards Copernicus' work, which he presented as mathematical fictions so as to avoid offending the religious sensibilities of his contemporaries.

## A DELAYED REACTION FROM THE CATHOLIC CHURCH

Aside from Osiander's cautious preface to Copernicus' book, the Catholic Church's delayed reaction - compared to that of the humanist reformers - is perhaps due to Copernicus' friendships with highly-placed figures in the Church. The Bishop of Chelmno Tiedemann Giese (1480-1550), the Cardinal of Capua Nikolaus von Schönberg (1472-1537), Secretary to Pope Clement VII (1506-1557) Johann Widmannstetter (1478-1534) and even the Pope himself took the time to personally encourage Copernicus to publish his work. Copernicus even dedicated his oeuvre to Pope Paul III (1468-1549). Alexander Farnese, the man who would become Paul III was himself a passionate humanist and a friend of Desiderius Erasmus and above all the man who initiated the Council of Trent and thus the Catholic Reformation. Copernicus takes care to mention in his dedication that mathematics should never be at the service of theology; the two disciplines should be free to develop independently. He furthermore reminds the reader that the greatest innovations are often met with outcry before their true value is later acknowledged.

However, while Copernicus' work initially provoked little reaction from the Catholic authorities, this was only because it was largely confined to intellectual circles. All that was to change when Galileo came along. Galileo defended both heliocentrism and the earth's motions as outlined by Copernicus and used these principles as the basis for his own work. Finally, Copernicus' work took centre stage, promoted by Galileo who refused to consider it as a mere hypothesis. Instead, he believed that it held the key to a true understanding of the world and the heavens. His refusal to back down enraged the Holy See, who summoned him before them in 1616, subsequently censoring his writings and placing Copernicus' work on the Church's list of banned heretical books. Galileo persisted, resulting in a spectacular trial in 1633 in which he was forced to retract his position. Copernicus' texts were only partially removed from the prohibited index in 1754 and were not completely liberated until 1835.

## THE COPERNICAN REVOLUTION

Despite the book being banned, the Copernican revolution had well and truly begun. Copernicus' work paved the way for new perspectives and new fields of study which were to result in great astronomical discoveries. While Galileo made heliocentrism and the earth's rotations famous, it was his contemporary Johannes Kepler - whose passion for optical science was matched only by his illustrious Italian counterpart Galileo - who used Copernicus' work alongside the Danish astronomer Tycho Brahe's precise observations to develop his laws of planetary motion. While investigating the apparent irregularity of planetary displacement speeds, he deduced that their orbits were not circular but elliptical. His three fundamental laws helped Isaac Newton developed his own universal law of gravitation which would in turn be challenged by Albert Einstein. Copernicus' hypotheses are therefore at the source of a torrent of discovery which would form the basis for modern-day astrophysics.

## LAWS OF MOTION

Both Johannes Kepler and Isaac Newton defined three fundamental laws of motion.

Kepler's laws are:

- Planets' orbits are elliptical, with the sun at one of two foci.
- A line joining a planet and the Sun sweeps out equal areas during equal intervals of time, meaning the speed at which a planet travels increases as it approaches the sun and decreases as it moves further away.
- The square of the orbital period is proportional to the cube of the semi-major axis (ie the radius of the broadest part of the ellipse) of its orbit. This means the distance between a planet and the sun can be calculated.

Focussing on Kepler's second law, Newton established three more fundamental laws:

- An object in a state of uniform motion will remain so in the absence of applied external force.
- If force is applied to a body, the body will accelerate in same direction as the force
- For every action there is an equal and opposite reaction.

These three laws together establish a principle of

universal gravitation. Following on from these laws, Einstein used the physics of Newton's three-dimensional universe to theorise his own four-dimensional model in which gravity is no longer a force which attracts but rather the effect of space-time curvature; planets are not attracted by a force but instead slide along the slope created by this curve.

# SUMMARY

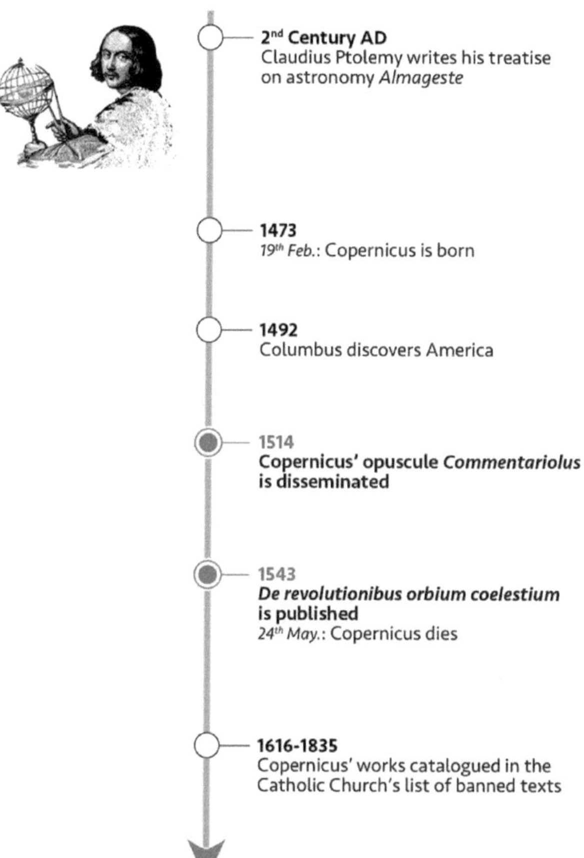

**2nd Century AD**
Claudius Ptolemy writes his treatise on astronomy *Almageste*

**1473**
*19th Feb.*: Copernicus is born

**1492**
Columbus discovers America

1514
**Copernicus' opuscule *Commentariolus* is disseminated**

1543
***De revolutionibus orbium coelestium* is published**
*24th May.*: Copernicus dies

**1616-1835**
Copernicus' works catalogued in the Catholic Church's list of banned texts



- Copernicus is born to a rich merchant family on 19 February 1473 in Toruń, Poland.

- Orphaned at a young age, Copernicus is adopted by his uncle Lucas Watzenrode, a powerful clergyman who allowed Copernicus to leave and pursue his studies at university in Krakow, Bologna and Padua.
- Copernicus is introduced to astronomy by two great masters of the field - one Polish, Albert Brudzewski and the other Italian, Domenico Maria Novara.
- He is appointed as canon at Frombork Cathedral, and takes on administrative and medical functions as well as writing an economic treatise and defending the city of Olsztyn in armed combat.
- Copernicus calls for a tower to be built next to Frombork Cathedral which allows him to pursue his passion for astronomy while fulfilling his ecclesiastical duties.
- In 1514 he writes a small book called *Commentariolus* in which he briefly outlines his new hypotheses: the Earth is neither stationary nor at the centre of the solar system. Instead, it rotates on its own axis and orbits the sun, as do the other planets.
- In 1543 his own disciple Rheticus has Copernicus' book *De revolutionibus orbium coelestium* published. In this work Copernicus demonstrates and explains all the observations and calculations which had led him to develop his heliocentric model of the solar system. The book is greeted with a mixed reception among Protestant reformationist circles. Copernicus dies in the same year.
- In 1616 Copernicus' book which had until then been well-received by the Catholic authorities was placed on the list of banned heretical texts following Galileo's more public work and its Copernican basis.
- The expression "the Copernican Revolution" is testament

to the importance of Copernicus' work in the field and evolution of astronomy, paving the way for ground-breaking discoveries from Johannes Kepler and Isaac Newton.

*We want to hear from you!*
*Leave a comment on your online library*
*and share your favourite books on social media!*

# FIND OUT MORE

## BIBLIOGRAPHY


* Biskup, M. (1974) Nouvelles recherches sur la biographie de Nicolas Copernic. *Revue d'histoire des sciences*. 27(4).
* Lebranchu, J. Y. (1934) *Écrits notables sur la monnaie (xvi<sup>e</sup> siècle), de Copernic à Davanzati*. Paris: Alcan.
* Lerner, M. P. (2006) Aux origines de la polémique anticopernicienne (II). *Revue des sciences philosophiques et théologiques*. Issue 3.
* Lipinski, E. (1961) *De Copernic à Stanislas Leszczynski*. Paris: Classiques de l'Économie et de la Population.
* Luminet, J. P. (2010) *Les bâtisseurs du ciel*. Paris: JC Lattès.
* Przypkowsk, T. (1951) Les instruments astronomiques de Nicolas Copernic. *L'astronomie*. Volume 65, p. 33.
* Szczeciniarz, J. J. (1998) *Copernic et la révolution copernicienne*. Paris: Flammarion.
* Thuan, T. X. (2009) *Le dictionnaire amoureux du Ciel et des Étoiles*. Paris: Plon/Fayard.
* Verdet, J. P. (No date) Nicolas Copernic. *Encyclopedia Universalis*. [Online]. [Accessed 25 October 2014]. Available from: <http://www.universalis.fr/encyclopedie/nicolas-copernic/>


## ADDITIONAL SOURCES


* Copernicus, N. (1995) *On the Revolutions of Heavenly Spheres (Great Minds Series)*. New York: Prometheus Books.
* Olson, R. G. (2006) *Science and Religion, 1450-1900: From*

*Copernicus to Darwin*. Maryland: Greenwood Press.
- Repcheck, J. (2008) *Copernicus' Secret: How the Scientific Revolution Began*. New York: Simon & Schuster, Inc.
- Wootton, D. (2016) *The Invention of Science: A New History of the Scientific Revolution*. New York: HarperCollins.

## ICONOGRAPHIC SOURCES

- Diagram of planetary trajectory according to Ptolemy's model. Royalty-free reproduction picture.
- Photo of a quadrant housed in the Copernicus Museum in Frombork. Royalty-free reproduction picture.
- Sketch of an armillary sphere taken from Diderot and d'Alembert's Encyclopédie. Royalty-free reproduction picture.
- Sketch of a triquetrum. Royalty-free reproduction picture.

## ICONOGRAPHY

- *Nicolas Copernic* (1580). Anonymous, housed at the District Museum of Toruń (Poland).
- *Nicolas Copernic (15th-16th century)*. Anonymous from a German school, library at the Paris Observatory, Paris (France).

www.50minutes.com

ISBN ebook: 9782806279194

ISBN paper: 9782806282316

Legal Deposit: D/2016/12603/246

Cover: © Primento

Digital conception by Primento, the digital partner of publishers.